From the pitch to the page

By Amanda Whiting

Copyright © 2017 by Amanda Whiting

For my family,
Thank you for loving and supporting me.

Thank you to my coaches and mentors who have guided me over the years

Scott Murray
Cherif Zein
Moji Oluwa
Nick Gumpert
James Ortega
The Futboleros
Alejo Escos
Sal Diaz
Sasha Khapsalis

From the Pitch to the Page. Copyright © 2017 by Amanda Whiting

All rights reserved. No part of this book may be reproduced in any form or by any electronic or mechanical means without the express written consent of the Author, except in the case of brief excerpts in critical reviews or articles.

All inquiries should be addressed to Amanda@SoccerPoetry.com

"In everything he did he had great success, because the LORD was with him."
1 Samuel 18:14

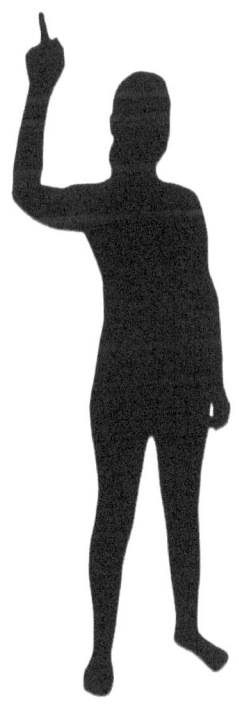

Table of Contents

Loving the Game
Feeling like a Boss
Team
Penalties
Struggles
Knowledge
Injuries
Victory
Tie
Defeat
Working Hard
Dealing with Disappointment
Proving Yourself
Coaches
New
Weather
Fitness
The Future

Loving the Game

Passion of Soccer

I woke up early
Went out to the field
This was a game
I was not going to yield
Our coach gives a speech
Before the game
No excuse to lose
No one to blame
As we jog to the center
My heart gives me a clue
That soccer was
What I was made to do

Experiments

I'm just playing
While I'm messing around I'm free
Even though it's just
The ball and me
Nobody's watching
No need for validation
No praise plea
Or ego inflation
Just trying new things
This is my lab
And there are more
Experiments to be had

Vigor

Passion in the game
It's an art
Gotta have it in your brain
But most in your heart
Play for yourself
For no parent or coach
Not for the political relationships
No award, trophy, and no gold broach
The dedication and enthusiasm
You would never trade or swap
The whistle may blow
But you never want to stop
The confidence in your skills
When playing the game you love and know
That feeling you worked for
You will never let go

Moment

Don't worry about College
Forget the national team
Don't worry about
Your far away dream
Play in the moment
No future or past
No self-sabotage
Make today's gold last
And then alas
When your time is near
You can look back
Without a fear
Of not achieving
What the world says you should do
Just focus on the passion
Which will take you through
Because it's all about
Living the game you love
And that's what I love
Over and above

Blessed

Pray consistent
Play consistent

Back

I've found my calling
It's the beautiful game
But sometimes I look back and wonder
Would I be the same
What if I did not play
And was just a normal girl
It scares me to think
About that being my world

Come On

I want to play great soccer
I love the beautiful game
And when I try and lose the ball
I'm okay with the blame

Style

Play passes
Hard on the ground
Quickly move
The ball around
Have good possession
While looking to the goal
Connect and work together
So we can play as a whole

Love the Game

A love of the game
Trade for nothing
The hard sacrifices
Smell of the grass
The role models
Proud feelings after triumph
Defeat feeling like death
Deeply enriching in a coach's knowledge
The bruises at the end of a day
Blood and tears
Late nights
Working your butt off at fitness
Caring for your teammates
The early morning drive
The pressure of a penalty
Sliding on turf
A mark to prove it
Scoring an important goal
The perfect save
Going to bed happy
Playing since you were little

Getting a harsh yellow card
Having vivid memories
The most prideful feeling
The coach's speech
Getting chosen as captain
Not getting praise for an assist
Being a boss
Getting new cleats
Loving the beautiful game

Feeling like a Boss

Playing soccer is a little bit like having a roll in a movie or play. The character you have on the field should not always be the same as your real personality in life. Often a successful footballer has to play the role of a confident, boastful superhero. Many of these poems in the "Feeling like a Boss" section are written from the perspective of this superhero. They may sound overly cocky, but they need to be that way to inspire a confident and winning mindset on the field. Off the field, a successful soccer player should be humble, friendly, and supportive of others.

Animal

Dribble down the line
Amazing pace
I'm the fastest
Horse in the race
Like a peacock
Burst with pride
Confidence
As I strut my stride
A little flash
I'm a show dog
I'm even merciless
As I jog
I'm a leader
Of the pack
Like a wolf
I attack
A tad bit
Of a ball hog
So fast in 2 seconds
Opponents in a fog

I think it's safe to say
At least
That I am an
Absolute beast

Magic

My touch is magic
Can't explain
Even Harry Potter
Hopes in vain
Tip of a wand
Is the tip of my shoe
Accept the wizardry
The ball and I can do
When I cut
And curve
Slash
And swerve
Like the TriWizard Champ
They all admire
Because I
I inspire

100

I'm balling
What a boss
Me is to win as
You is to loss
Showmanship
Swag
Baller's out of the bag
They all respect
I run this show
They are the grass
And I'm about to mow
The game hasn't started
And it's already done
Cause they all know it
I'm one hundred and ONE

Watch

It's just a ball
But it's so much more
I can volley, pass, shoot,
Watch me score

Watch Defenders Be Amazed

We work wondrous works
When the ball's at our feet
The defense doth dour
Due to power of defeat
Because we're the better ballers
Boss best number one
Amazing things accomplished already
And still more to come

CASH IN

Punt
Up so far so high
The ball has wings
Watch it fly
My touch lands it softly at my foot
Like glue
And Silkily
Sticks to my shoe
Then I am a spinstress
Through the defenders I weave
A treasure chest of greatness
And I have the key
Inside out *cut* around
They double team me
But I easily bound
And curve and swerve
Without a sound
The only thing I'll lose
Is my defender
The technique superb

So crisp the splendor
I'm on *fire*
They all admire
The grit the desire
My skills surprise like a trip wire
Confidence
So **bold** and brave
Borderline cocky
But it's ok
Pace
Both on and off the ball
Scouts all think they've seen it all
But no
They're wrong
So incorrect
Because every time I shoot
The ball finds the net
Running so *fast*
I refuse to lose
On your ego
I'll leave a **bruise**
I fake a shot
A body check
I fly past them

Without a sweat
Lebron on the court
Is like me on the field
This is NOT just a game
I am not going to yield
To the other team's dream
Of being supreme
The joy
The passion
My skills
I'm slashing
I finish
We win
My soccer
CASH IN

Juggle

Touch touch
Keep it in the air
Up up
Time to add a little FLAIR
Don't want chocolate or vanilla
Give me strawberry sorbet
Creativity when I juggle
A pop or a fizz when I play
I need something
Inspiring to eat
A rainbow a headstall
A trick and a treat
Oh so inventive
Its neat nifty and new
And there are endless possibilities
Of what you can do

Fast or Last

Hat tricks on hat tricks
The crowd's going wild
I'm all the opponents'
Fears compiled
All the expectations
I will exceed
Sprinting so quickly
Can't fathom the speed
The technique
Passing receiving trapping
Another goal
Everyone's clapping

Team

Together

From them
To us

Hotel

We fool around
After we won
Ding dong ditch
And then we run

Exclusive

They walk away
Don't like me it seems
But we'll have to collaborate
And fake that we're a team

Close

Work together
I always beam
Love you guys
You're my sisters

Woken

They help me wake up
At 5 a.m.
By jumping on my bed
So thanks to them

Fly

Up up
And away
Off to score
A goal today

Penalties

Make

The pressure is on
It's my time to shine
Keeper's on
The goal line
I set up the ball
On a damp patch
Only I can decide
If we win the match
I stare down the goalie
Everything is at stake
But both her and I
Know I'm going to make
Top left corner
Scarlet, crimson, cardinal
It's a bulls eye
And the arrow is my ball
Victory
My immense success
I've sought and found
Oh my sweet conquest

Miss

Wish I could redo it
Regret on the mind
That opportunity
Was one of a kind
My team worked hard
Until the last whistle blow
I'm sorry
Next time
I'll keep
My penalty low

Struggles

Break

Coach says we get rest
After a hard day
But I want to get back on the field
And play
I miss my teammates
The confidence and power
I can hardly stand it
And it's only been an hour

Occupied

No social life
"Sorry, can't go"
I have soccer
But you already know

Just a Helper

Amazing assist
I pulled off that goal
She needed my help
We did it as a whole
But when we run back
She gets all the credit
What about that perfect ball
I threaded
She gets all the hugs
Her victory to claim
Her tremendous triumph
She won us the game
Finished her opportunity
Celebrates with class
And I'm just the girl
Who made the pass

Question

Would my question
Be too stupid to say
He explained it
But I still don't get how to play
I want it repeated
Even though it was explained well
Would it lead to annoyance or anger
I can't tell
Don't want to go back
And not know what to do
But when asking
Will it look like I have low IQ
Maybe he'll answer
In the flick of the dime
So I'll take that risk
And ask one more time

Hair

The rats nest
On the top of my head
Looks like
I just got out of bed
There are knots EVERYWHERE
I've used spray
Believe it or not
I brush it everyday

SWITCH?!

I don't want to play there
I don't want to go
I've been playing this position my whole life!
How will I know
What to do
And what is coach thinking

When he changes my spot

Without even blinking

More Gold Less Green

Number 1 in the world
They brought back the gold
So why do these ladies
Have less to hold
Much worse conditions
Victims of the gender pay gap
It's unacceptable
What is this crap

Vexation

Everyone's worried about scouts
And it makes me mad
Because though they try to impress
When they stress it makes them play bad

More

I'm so hungry
I need food
Snacks on snacks
Being ravishly chewed
Pizza pasta popcorn
Edibles of all kind
Carb Loading tonight
Before I unwind

Knowledge

Click

Key to lock
Password to phone
Like knowledge
When your mind gets blown

Knowledge

His teaching so new
Rare as blue newt
Fresh as the news
Every time learn something new
Could learn from dusk 'til noon
Correct what you thought you knew

Comprehend

Got to have lessons and learning
To be tutored and taught
I desire knowledge and knowhow
And I want it a lot
Review and reprogram
Corrections and getting caught
I need insight and intelligence
And that's what I got

Eh feedback

The insight
Tonight
Was alright

Injuries

Hurt

Sitting on the side
Dying to play
Just to touch the ball
Oh the amount I would pay
To run
Like I'm running from society
All the stress school and anxiety
To shoot
To score
And so much
More
To be freed
From the cage
All the opponents
I would upstage
The boss
Trapped in the brace
The talent
Held behind the lace
What teammates

Take for granted
Is what others
Long for
A speechless tiger
Trying to let out a roar
The pain of an injury
Or the pain of not playing
One step on the pitch?
That's what I'm weighing
Not for the glory
Just for the joy
It's killing me inside
Am I life's toy
To break
And never play
This is not my future
I do pray
All the training
Work put in
Blood and tears
Scabs scatter my skin
I would not trade this
for anything
Just let me tie that

Magista cleat string
Forget diamonds and ferraris
I just want to be healed
Anyone
Just let me back on the field!
My need to play
Is insane
I just want to play
My beautiful game

Stuck

I go head to head
With the defender
Little do I know
She's about to render
My prospective capacity
To compete
And strip away
The spheres tango
With my feet
Inspiring all
It was our galvanizing groove
But now I
Can hardly move

Injured Again

Take two steps forward
Then three back

Dust and Rust

First practice back
Trying to shake off the dust
But what do I lack
I feel like there's this rust
Got to get in my groove
But it's been so long
Since I have moved
That I don't feel strong

Done

Go
Blocked out
I'm playing
What
Bye
Practice
Strength
Built
Building
Go
Long coming
Keep going
Not now
Moment
Time
Game
Go
Accelerate
Fast
Faster

Rep
Run
Touches
Go
In
Out
Ah
Help me
Slowing
Ouch
Uw
Awful
Agitating
Aggravating
Go
Stop
Come
Time
What
Hello
Now
Go
What
Hello

Go
Help
Go
Go

Ice Bath

The ice is freezing
My legs have turned red
There's numbing in my toes
And tingling in my head
It's colder than the North Pole
Temperature is 42
But taking this bath
Is what I must do
To not be injured
Be totally healed
Get back to my team
And back on the field

Played

Heart and soul
Overall throughout
This was my future
Without a doubt
Pain overcoming
Injury why
Loved the game
Two reasons to die
Hard work was done
But because of this knee
I can't play the game
Now because it's playing me

Careful

All the hard sacrifices
That they don't know
Have to be careful
Everywhere I go
But sometimes
It stops fun
Because I've got to beware of injury
Unlike everyone

Victory

Yeet

If the ball's at our feet
You're already beat
Skills with the cleat
Amazing athletes
Fast as a heartbeat
Take a seat
We'll throw heat
You can't even compete
Blatant defeat
Victory is so sweet
Repeat

Triumph

I love the feeling
Of success
The goal
A symbol of playing my best
I tell the ref
My number with pride
I point to God
As I stride
Back to my team
And we celebrate
My triumphing goal
That was truly great

#1

Peak
But no **drop**
Touch the stars
And don't **stop**
Harvest the reward
Like a **crop**
The climb was hard
But we're at the **top**

Victory

We just beat Sharks!
Work paid off a ton
Can you believe it was
Two to one
Played physical tactical
Technically super smart
But most of all
We played with our hearts

W

Never lose
Ya I refuse
Genius of Shakespeare
No Ls here
Fastest horse in the race
Vigorous dribbling pace
They all wish to acquire
Cause my shot is fire
Singlehandedly won
And I've just begun

Tie

Tie

Why can't we score
All games end in a tie
Got strong defense
That can deny
But somehow
No matter how many chances we get
We can't seem to put the ball
In the back of the net

Draw

They all seem happy
About another tie
But not me
I'm not satisfied
Got a desire to win
And to win is to succeed
Winning's not a want
Winning is a need!

Defeat

Loss

Suffer the pain
Of a defeat
Can't go back
What happened feet
The hours
The training
In shine
Or while raining
Feels like a waste
Plain taste of a loss
Buffooned and baffled
From beast and the boss
What happened out there
Utter shell shock
Left it all on the field
But still want to wind back the clock
They say learn to lose
But it's hard to embrace
That one moment
Strike of their lace

But there's another day
Lift up your chin
I'll get another
Chance to win

Failure

Refuse
To lose
Again
The loss
Has cost
My pride
I can't stand this feeling
My ego needs some healing
We need to win the next game

Want

It's unprofessional
Lack of focus
From when we warmed up
That's why we played like bogus
Got to have desire
To stick out from the rest
Or else you won't
Play your best

Working Hard

Work

'Til you're tired
Exhausted
Out of breath
Blood and tears now
Trophies
Later

Dedicated

Like.
No.
Other.

Grind
Dedicated to Moji Oluwa

Got to go to the grind
Gonna work hard and get strong
Put in the time
So I can prove them all wrong

Dealing with Disappointment

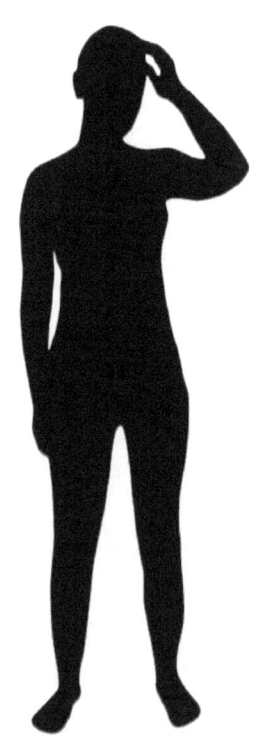

Shame

During the talk
I'm called out
Out of the crowd
Without a doubt
Because how I played on the weekend
How I blew the game
If I could just be more fit
There'd be no more blame

Delusion

Is my swag delusion
Maybe I am not all that
Is it just plain confusion
Am I a know-it-all brat
What if it's all
In my mind
And when I touch the ball
It looks everything but refined
I fantasize I'm the best
But conceivably all this pride
On my cocky chest
Is just one immense lie

Car Lecture

Ok I get it!
I lost the ball and looked slow
I was THERE on the field
So I know
I don't get how to improve
I just don't get what to do
And I could probably play better
If I knew
Of course I want to do good
I'm trying here
But I just keep messing up
And the end doesn't look near
I understand that
I'm not playing my best
But it's harder
Than you'd guess

Looking Back

Got to pick myself up
It wasn't just me
Should I blame my bad fitness
Or was it my knee
Try to stay positive
But my mind it crossed
If I had tried harder
We wouldn't have lost

Out

Why did you take me out
I thought I did well
Felt I was effective
But now I can't tell
My sub went in
And I just couldn't hide
My disappointment
When I sat on the side

Pressure

How many chances
Until one is too much
Getting nervous
To show my silky touch
Afraid of mistakes
But all I do is stress
About getting cut
From the rest

Garment of Shame

My unwashed penny
Draped around my chest
An exhibition
Of not playing my best

Bench

Once again I sit
On the bench under a tent
This has happened every game
Since the last tournament
Don't know what to do
Where did I go wrong
In the coach's head
It's where I belong
But it's not what I want
This is not okay!
To prove myself
I need to go out and play

Scarce

Creativity has run dry
Not one single drop
Used to be tricky and skillful
Used to be on the top
But it feels like I'm on a road
That only goes one way
I've lost my passion
And will to play

Proving Yourself

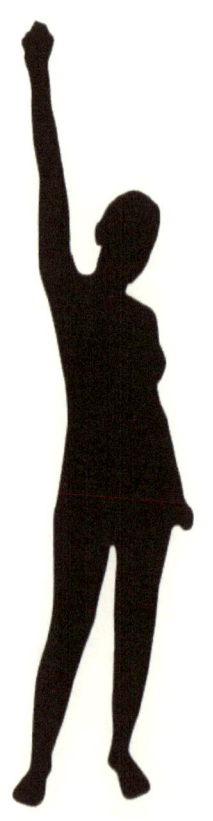

Take 2

Got another chance
To prove myself today
Going to relax
And have fun while I play
I'll move the ball
With no delay
I'll shoot like a beast
And watch their defense decay
Not the mention
All the words I'll say
Descriptive ones
Unlike pass here and hey
Shot number 2
And oh I do pray
That I won't throw
This opportunity away

Roll

Redeemed myself
I played so well
Just one look
And you could tell
Strutted like a peacock
'Cause that's the way I stride
All that confidence
No one could hide
Was hesitant at the beginning
But now I'm at the top
Still on my way up
And I'm not going to stop

Own

Don't let the rats
Eat your cheese

Tryout

Butterflies
Sweaty palms
Nervous thoughts
Trying to stay calm
About to audition
What will they be looking for
Gonna play great
So they'll remember me more
I step out on the pitch
And I get a sense
That I'm about
To impress

Soar

I think I'm playing great
I'm starting to finally grow
Was feeling mediocre
But I flew off my plateau

Coaches

Instructor

Mentor
No snore
Or bore
He's more
The best
I'm impressed
Passed test
I'm blessed
His team
Is my dream
I'd beam
Joyful scream

Bye

What happened to you
How should I know
What I should do
Where did you go
I want everyone to see
How amazing you are
But how can it be
That you have moved so far
You were my best coach
It all happened so fast
Trying to play like you taught me
Even though it's in the past

Shhh

I know when to go to the middle
And get out to the wide
I can think for myself
So stop yelling on the side
It's confusing
And distracting me
But I guess that's one thing
You can't see

Comprehension

You put effort into the team
Your knowledge helps me grow
When you instruct me
With all the things you know

Mentor

Dedicated to Scott Murray

Knowledge overflows
The vast immensity he knows
Coaching power overthrows
So you don't want to oppose
Helps accomplish dreams
When I see him I beam
And it seems
He can't get beat by a team
Encourages being bold
Pearls of wisdom to behold
Accurately scolds
His feedback is gold
And not to mention
Brilliant comprehension
Cares and gives attention
Deals with soccer parent tension
Knows when to yell
Answers back on his cell
Prominent as a bell
His team always does well

They win every gold broach
From other teams he'll poach
Happy to approach
He's the ideal coach

Inspiration

My heart got crushed
He's not my coach
Pain like no other
Doesn't even approach
I loved his insight
All the knowledge
Helped girls develop
Then to college
Trained like nobody's business
We started to win
We felt like champions
And we had just begin
In the short time
We had worked together
I could already feel myself
Getting better
You were my favorite coach
Time seemed so rushed
And now that you're gone
I will miss you so much

Teach
Dedicated to Cherif Zein

What an amazing coach
Working with him is a thrill
Sunday Sushi Session
Teaches us skill
At shooting clinic
Get to work on my shot
Always improving with Cherif
I love to get taught

Coach
Dedicated to Nick Gumpert

You instruct, train, and teach
Us so much
Show us width and depth
How to have a silky touch
Spacing is key
Weak side further back
How to transition
From defense to attack
I love being on your team
And competing for my position
You're a great coach
Filled with understanding and ambition

New

New pet

I'm the shiny new toy
Honestly it feels GREAT
Coach says it's cool
When I am late
It's fine if I mistouch
Not one single yell
Everything I do
Is considered swell

New Girl

I ask the girl
Who is new
What position do you play?
Me too!
So you're from an elite team
While I've heard that a lot
So let's go to the field
And see what you got...

New Coach

On the block
Will you live
Up to the talk
Or
Will you just
Be there for show
Or
Will you help us
Expand and grow

New Cleats

My babies
I'll make sure you're always clean
I will rub you and polish you
Before we go out to the green
The way you look and feel
Oh the perfection
I can practically
See my reflection
I'm completely ready to play
And kick some hiney
Because my new cleats
Are nice and shiny

Weather

Drizzle

Leading up
The practice hype
That the rain has stopped
Off the field I'll wipe
The water that
Kept me from playing
No more rain
I'm pleading praying
Wishing hoping
Wanting willing
To stop what kept me
From with the ball filling
The net
That would bring glory to my team
Coach would be proud
Words of encouragement and beam
Just want to hear the knowledge
That he would speak
But the water keeps pouring
Week after week

Cancelled

Could be balling and scoring
But this rain keeps on pouring
Just want one practice when it's hot
To be critiqued and taught
Pearls of wisdom I'd know
But that water does flow
And on goes the rain
My joy does drain
Oh This weather of grey
Kills my ability to play

Heat

The sun beats down
Upon my head
I looked on to the distance
The heat waves steadily spread
I can't keep going
Try to be a tough athlete
But I just cannot
Handle this heat

Fitness

Gassed

Got to play faster
Got to have speed
That quick mentality
Is what I need
But how to get fit
I don't know
My body says stop
But my mind MUST say go
Have to get to the ball
With no delay
But I'm worried I'll be tired
For the next play
Sacrifice
Comfort for pain
So I can be a BEAST
On the field again

Notice

I'm fit
And that's why I play fast
But then I wonder
How long will it last
Try to run faster
Try to stand out
Then I'll get
Noticed by a scout
But if I'm not fit
Will I be written down
As just another girl
Jogging around

Get it

I am fit
I don't quit
So legit
No limit

The Future

One Day

It's hard to play
When I know one day
I'll have to give
It all away
My muscles weak
I will grow old
The work won't stay
This was my gold
The late nights
Blood and tears
Fade away
Disappear
Will be hard to run
Then to walk
No left effort to
Lead and talk
I'll see the ball
And die to play
But isn't dying
What will keep me away

My bones in pain
My heart is too
The beautiful game
That I once knew

Go

Don't stop playing
Don't move on
You're an egg that's hatching
Soon to be a swan
Even if people don't get
The magic you do
Don't let it
Ever stop you

Soon

It's a moving train
With a fast rate
And I better hop on
Or it will be too late

Stay

I want the game in my life
Forever on
I'd be at the peak of my game
But then it'll be gone

A word of closing for all the soccer players out there reading this

Stay positive, have fun, love the game, take risks, work hard, and have confidence!

AMANDA WHITING has played soccer her entire life and started writing these poems as a way to chronicle the highs and lows of the sport. After a while, a pretty large assemblage of poetry started to collect, and that's when she had the idea to turn them into this book. Amanda continues to pursue her passion as a writer and player at LA Premier FC and hopes to inspire younger players as a coach some day.

www.ingramcontent.com/pod-product-compliance
Lightning Source LLC
Chambersburg PA
CBHW032042290426
44110CB00012B/921